*Retaining Walls*

Schiffer Publishing Ltd
4880 Lower Valley Road, Atglen, PA 19310 USA

# Retaining Walls

# A Building Guide and Design Gallery

## Tina Skinner & The National Concrete Masonry Association

**Managing Editor**
– Tina Skinner–
**Editor**
–Lindy McCord–
**Technical writer/editor**
– R. Lance Carter, P.E.–
**Designer**
– John Cheek–
**Cover Design**
– Bruce Waters–

Library of Congress Cataloging-in-Publication Data:

Skinner, Tina.
  Retaining Walls: a building guide and design gallery / by Tina Skinner & the National Concrete Masonry Association.
    p. cm.
  ISBN 0-7643-1836-5 (Paperback)
1. Retaining walls—Design and construction. I. National Concrete Masonry Association. II. Title.
TA770.S55 2003
624.1'64—dc21
                    2003000528

Type set in Kabel Bd/Zurich BT

ISBN: 0-7643-1836-5
Printed in China

Published by Schiffer Publishing Ltd.
4880 Lower Valley Road
Atglen, PA 19310
Phone: (610) 593-1777; Fax: (610) 593-2002
E-mail: Info@schifferbooks.com
Please visit our web site catalog at
**www.schifferbooks.com**
We are always looking for people to write books on new and related subjects. If you have an idea for a book, please contact us at the above address.

This book may be purchased from the publisher.
Include $3.95 for shipping.
Please try your bookstore first.
You may write for a free catalog.

In Europe, Schiffer books are distributed by
Bushwood Books
6 Marksbury Avenue
Kew Gardens
Surrey TW9 4JF England
Phone: 44 (0) 20 8392 8585
Fax: 44 (0) 20 8392 9876
E-mail: Bushwd@aol.com
Free postage in the UK. Europe: air mail at cost.

# Contents

Introduction ..................................................... 6
Chapter 1 – History ...................................... 7
Chapter 2 – Basics ..................................... 12
    Selecting a Retaining Wall Product ............ 12
    Backfill Options ........................................... 13
        Granular, select Fill ............................ 14
        Fine-grained, Non-select Fill ................ 14
    Grading and Drainage ............................... 16
    Compaction ............................................... 21
    Geosynthetics ............................................ 22
        Geotextiles Filter ................................. 23
        Geogrid and Geotextile Soil Reinforcement ......... 23

Chapter 3 – Segmental Retaining Wall Maintenance
and Aesthetics ........................................... 25
    Maintenance and Cleaning ........................ 25
    Vegetation – Selection and Placement ....... 26
        Plantings and Trenching – Interaction with
        Soil Reinforcement ............................. 33
    Tiered, Multi-level Segmental Retaining Walls .......... 33
Chapter 4 - Segmental Retaining Wall Construction ...... 36
    Planning .................................................... 37
    Construction ............................................... 37
Chapter 5 – Segmental Retaining Wall Construction
(A Step-by-Step Guide) ............................... 39
    Excavation ................................................. 39
    Foundation Soil and Leveling Pad Construction ......... 40
    Drainage Pipe Installation .......................... 42
    Setting, Leveling, and Backfilling the First Course
        of SRW Units ...................................... 42
    Installing Successive Courses of SRWs ...... 45
    Placement and Tensioning of Reinforcement
        and Placement of Backfill .................... 46
    Capping and Finish Grading ...................... 53
Chapter 6 – Image Gallery ............................ 56
References .................................................... 127
Contributors ................................................. 128

# Introduction

This gallery and installation guide for segmental retaining walls was created through the joint efforts of the National Concrete Masonry Association and Schiffer Publishing. This book provides the homeowner and residential contractor with many beautiful examples of segmental retaining wall concepts and installations. The reader is provided with industry recognized installation guidelines and general project considerations that ensure the longevity and performance of the landscape investment.

The information contained within is based on conventional engineering principles and construction practices demonstrated on a large number of segmental retaining wall structures in North America over the past twenty years. The objective of this book is to provide basic knowledge about segmental retaining walls in a systematic step-by-step process using widely accepted construction practices.

This book will also provide a basic understanding of how segmental retaining walls perform and how the consumer can understand what is important when considering segmental retaining walls. The knowledge and experience within this book is developed from an industry of successful segmental retaining wall system producers and suppliers.

The National Concrete Masonry Association invites consumers to preview the vast number of aesthetic and geometric alternatives available, and hopes that the public will benefit from the experiences of our landscape industry.

# Chapter 1
# History

When considering an investment in a retaining wall system, it is often important to understand the history of the product. Retaining walls have been around since the first time people determined it was beneficial to hold something back. The first retaining walls were often constructed using stones, rubble, wood or other material that could be easily stacked to create a wall. As time passed, the knowledge gained from trial and error led to innovative construction practices. It was soon learned that various and readily-available materials could be introduced into the soil fill that is placed behind the wall facing, allowing for the construction of taller, more stable structures. Hence, the concept of reinforced soil walls was born.

In fact, the concept of segmental walls and reinforced soil is surprisingly old. The Ziggurats of Babylonia (i.e., Tower of Babel) were built some 2,500 to 3,000 years ago using soil-reinforcing methods very similar to those that are described in this book for reinforced soil segmental retaining walls [Ref. 1]. Early versions of reinforced soil walls often consisted of thinly placed soil lifts with intermittent layers of fabric or branches. One such wall built using this early version of soil reinforcement was The Great Wall of China. The Great Wall of China was built using a mixture of clay and gravel reinforced with tamarisk branches [Ref. 1]. Today's segmental retaining wall systems can be considered an advancement of this age-old technology.

The use of interlocking concrete wall units was first introduced in the 1960s with a system known as concrete crib walls. The segmental retaining walls illustrated throughout this book are an advancement in modular block wall technology and provide an architecturally acceptable concrete facing system that can be machine made or cast without the need for internal steel reinforcement. The use of segmental retaining wall units became prominent in the U.S. in the mid-1980s, and shortly thereafter, construction began to incorporate geosynthetics and larger wall heights became possible. Segmental retaining walls have grown rapidly ever since.

As demonstrated by the many beautiful wall options contained in this book, a variety of proprietary segmental retaining wall units are available. The units are available in a variety of sizes, shapes and interlocking mechanisms. Since segmental retaining wall units are made of concrete, there are no restrictions on their size and shape. Most proprietary units are 3 to 24 inches in height, 6 to 30 inches in width and 6 to 72 inches in length. The smaller units are readily available for the homeowner, while wall contractors more often utilize larger units.

NOTE: THE UNITS PRESENTED ARE PROPRIETARY AND/OR PATENTED SYSTEMS

Examples of Commercially Available Segmental Retaining Wall Units.
[Ref. 1]

A segmental retaining wall project is only limited by imagination, product structural capacity, and budget. Wall applications include, but are not limited to:

- Landscaping walls (flower beds, planter walls, sidewalk and driveway accents)
- Structural walls for grade separation
- Waterway channelization
- Parking area support
- Roadway and highway structures

Segmental retaining walls are viable alternatives to other retaining wall structures. As with any retaining wall, segmental retaining walls require one to recognize project requirements, product limitations and aesthetic possibilities in order to ensure success. With a segmental retaining wall project in mind, the remainder of this book will guide one through common, practical project considerations and construction practices.

Some retaining wall units have an old-world, castle-like appearance.
*Courtesy of Pacific Precast Products*

*Courtesy of Anchor Wall Systems*

*Courtesy of Risi*
*Stone Systems*

Some units are tumbled to give an older, rustic appearance.

*Courtesy of Risi Stone Systems*

*Courtesy of Allan Block Corporation*

Chapter 2
# Basics

## Selecting a Retaining Wall Product

A segmental retaining wall system is a unique hybrid of structural performance and quality aesthetics that are achieved with specialized concrete units. The units are machine made from portland cement, water, suitable mineral aggregates, and other concrete additives such as color pigments and chemical additives. Segmental retaining wall suppliers are devoted to the long-term performance of their system and can assist in selecting a product that is appropriate for your project.

In many parts of the country, local building codes require a permit for any retaining wall constructed over a specified height. This height varies by area and typically ranges between four to six feet. It is important that one comply with local building codes or neighborhood covenants when determining what type of retaining wall system to install.

When a project is required to comply with local building codes or is part of residential or commercial project specifications, the units can be required to meet minimum industry standards for the manufacture of segmental retaining wall units. Segmental retaining wall units are readily manufactured to comply with ASTM International standards. ASTM C 1372, *Standard Specification for Segmental Retaining Wall Units* establishes minimum criteria assuring that units are uniform in weight, meet minimum dimensional tolerances, meet specified minimum strength, and comply with durability-features. If required by a local municipality or type of application, your system supplier can provide the necessary information demonstrating their product complies with industry standards.

It is important to note that the minimum requirements set forth by ASTM are not generally applied to units utilized within the homeowner or do-it-yourself market. These products, often called garden wall systems, planter wall units, or similar landscape accent products often comply with ASTM C 1372, but are not governed by municipal or site-specific project specifications. Consult with local suppliers and municipal officials to determine the requirements for your area.

With so many sizes, shapes and aesthetic options, how can one choose? This question can readily be answered with the aid of your local supplier. Your local supplier is a great resource in assisting with product selection. Several factors will assist both you and your supplier in selecting the right product.

First, segmental retaining wall units provide several functions:

• Serve as a structural element, retaining soil and prevent lateral movement or overturning of the wall.
• Provide a formwork so fill can be placed and compacted behind the segmental retaining wall unit.
• Offer aesthetic options that meet architectural and appearance needs of your project.
• Provide stability to adjacent soil behind the segmental wall unit and protect retained soil from erosion due to water flow.

The retaining wall height will have a significant influence on product selection. This is because the applied load or how much resistance to load a wall can accommodate is a direct function of wall height, type of unit, and wall geometry. A greater height means greater load, thus the wall units will generally need to be larger as the wall height increases. However, many segmental retaining wall systems can readily incorporate soil reinforcement that allows the construction of much taller walls with small wall units. Reinforced soil segmental retaining walls have been successively constructed to heights of 50 feet and greater.

Segmental retaining wall systems can be subdivided into two categories: 1) Conventional gravity walls and 2) Reinforced soil walls.

Conventional segmental retaining walls rely only on the weight of the units to prevent the wall from sliding or overturning (toppling) about the bottom (toe) of wall. Since the units are placed without mortar, (commonly referred to as dry-stacking) the shear capacity (resistance to sliding) between individual units is an important component. Without this resistance to movement, the units will not work together as a coherent mass, and the wall

## ENGINEERING PROPERTIES OF SOILS [Ref. NCMA DMSRW, 2nd Edition]

| Typical Names of Soil Groups | USCS Group Symbols | Permeability when Compacted | Shearing Strength when Compacted and Saturated | Compressibility when Compacted and Saturated | Workability as a Construction Material |
|---|---|---|---|---|---|
| Well-graded gravels, gravel-sand mixtures, little or no fines | GW | Pervious | excellent | negligible | excellent |
| Poorly graded gravels, gravel-sand mixtures, little or no fines | GP | very pervious | good | negligible | good |
| Silty gravels, poorly graded gravel-sand-silt mixtures | GM | semipervious to impervious | good | negligible | good |
| Clayey gravels, poorly graded gravel-sand-clay mixtures | GC | impervious | good to fair | very low | good |
| Well-graded sands, gravelly sands, little or no fines | SW | pervious | excellent | negligible | excellent |
| Poorly graded sands, gravelly sands, little or no fines | SP | pervious | good | very low | fair |
| Silty sands, poorly graded sand-silt mixtures | SM | semipervious to impervious | good | low | fair |
| Clayey sands, poorly graded sand-clay mixtures | SC | impervious | good to fair | low | good |
| Inorganic silts and very fine sands, rock flour, silty or clayey fine sands with slight plasticity | ML | semipervious to impervious | fair | medium | fair |
| Inorganic clays of low to medium plasticity, gravelly clays, sandy clays, silty clays, lean clays | CL | impervious | fair | medium | good to fair |

Table 1

The USCS provides some basic tests that permit the contractor to quickly evaluate the water retention capacity of the project soils [Ref. 10]. An installer can use these same tests to understand the types of soils available for their project. In doing so, beneficial knowledge is gained that will be assist your system supplier in selecting a wall system best suited for your project.

Snake Test - Assists in identifying clay content

• Moisten a small soil sample until the point at which it is soft, but not muddy or sticky.
• Roll the soil sample into a thread (snake) between your hands.
• The greater the length of the thread, and the more it can be rolled without breaking, is an indication of clay content. The longer the thread, the greater the clay content.

Patty Test - Assists in evaluating water retention (holding) capacity

• Mix sufficient water with a soil sample to create a putty-like consistency.
• Form the soil sample into a patty and let it dry completely.

• After completely drying, break the soil patty. The more effort required to break the patty with your fingers is an indication of greater water retention. The greater the water holding capacity the less suitable the soil is for wall fill. Silt and sand soils will break easily, while clay soils will not break as easily.

Shake Test - Assists in identifying water-holding capacity when exposed to shaking (dilatency test)

• With a soil sample in hand, add a tablespoon of water. The soil sample is to be soft but not muddy or sticky.
• Shake the sample in the closed palm of your hand a few times.
• If the soil is fine sand, the water will come to the surface of the soil.
• If the soil is silt or clay, little or no water will come to the surface.
• Squeeze the soil sample between your fingers. If sand, the moisture will disappear.
• Silty soil will not readily dissipate the water.
• The moisture will not disappear if the soil is clay.

An engineer classifies the water holding ability of a soil in terms of the Plasticity Index (P.I.). The larger the P.I., the greater the water holding capacity of soil, the greater the fines content, and the more clay or silt present with in the soil.

For larger retaining wall projects where designs require specific soil types, the wall should be constructed with materials that meet specified soil particle gradations.

The National Concrete Masonry Association recommends that segmental retaining wall backfill comply with the following gradation and a Plasticity Index (P.I.) less than 20:

| Sieve Size | Percent Passing |
| --- | --- |
| 4 inch | 100-75 |
| No. 4 | 100-20 |
| No. 40 | 0-60 |
| No. 200 | 0-35 |

When soil reinforcement is required as part of the segmental retaining wall, the maximum particle size of the soil should be limited to 3/4 inch. Soil with particle sizes greater than 3/4 inch require the geosynthetic soil reinforcement supplier to quantify the impact of these larger particles on the reinforcement's design strength.

The NCMA gradation allows for a wide range of soil types including fine-grained soils. If a granular, select material is utilized, the following gradation satisfies NCMA requirements and conforms to many highway transportation requirements:

| Sieve Size | Percent Passing |
| --- | --- |
| 4 inch | 100 |
| No. 40 | 0-60 |
| No. 200 | 0-15 |

A Plasticity Index (P.I.) less than 6.

Again, when soil reinforcement is required as part of the segmental retaining wall, the maximum particle size of the soil should be limited to 3/4 inch. Soil with particle sizes greater than 3/4 inch require the geosynthetic soil reinforcement supplier to quantify the impact of these larger particles on the reinforcement's design strength.

# Grading and Drainage

One of the most important decisions that can be made during layout and construction of a retaining wall is how surface water (rainwater, water from down spouts, runoff from adjacent surfaces) and subsurface water (groundwater, water that infiltrates the soil from other sources) will be handled. Grading and drainage considerations are critical in the long-term performance of a retaining wall. Water represents the most common factor in most performance problems with retaining walls.

The presence of water within and behind a retaining wall can lead to hydrostatic pressures. Hydrostatic pressure is an additional lateral pressure imposed upon the wall system during the presence of water. Hydrostatic pressure is in addition to lateral pressures (load) from the soil fill and other external load (traffic from roads or driveway, pedestrian traffic, maintenance equipment, and etc.)

The simplest way to understand why water has such a significant impact on wall stability is to compare the lateral load applied by water to that applied by the soil alone. Most soil utilized in retaining wall construction imposes a lateral pressure equal to 1/4 to 1/2 of the vertical pressure imposed by the self-weight of soil. Conversely, water imposes a lateral pressure equal to its vertical pressure.

In terms of actual calculated pressure, the total lateral earth pressure for select granular fill on a 5-foot high wall is approximately 420 lbs. per foot of wall. The total lateral earth pressure for the same wall with complete hydrostatic pressure is approximately 990 lbs. per foot of wall. Thus, the wall with full hydrostatic pressure must resist more than two times the total lateral earth pressure.

## Grading

Control of surface water during and after construction is very important. It is best to grade behind the wall such that all surface water is directed away from the wall. However, this is not always possible and would impose many restrictions upon aesthetic options and site geometry. When surface water is directed towards a retaining wall, a drainage swale is one method of directing this water away. A drainage swale is a small drainage channel or ditch placed directly at the top of and behind the retaining wall. The drainage swale will carry water away from the wall minimizing the potential for water to overtop (run down the front of) the wall or pond behind the wall and infiltrate into the wall fill. Example drainage swales are shown in Figure 2.

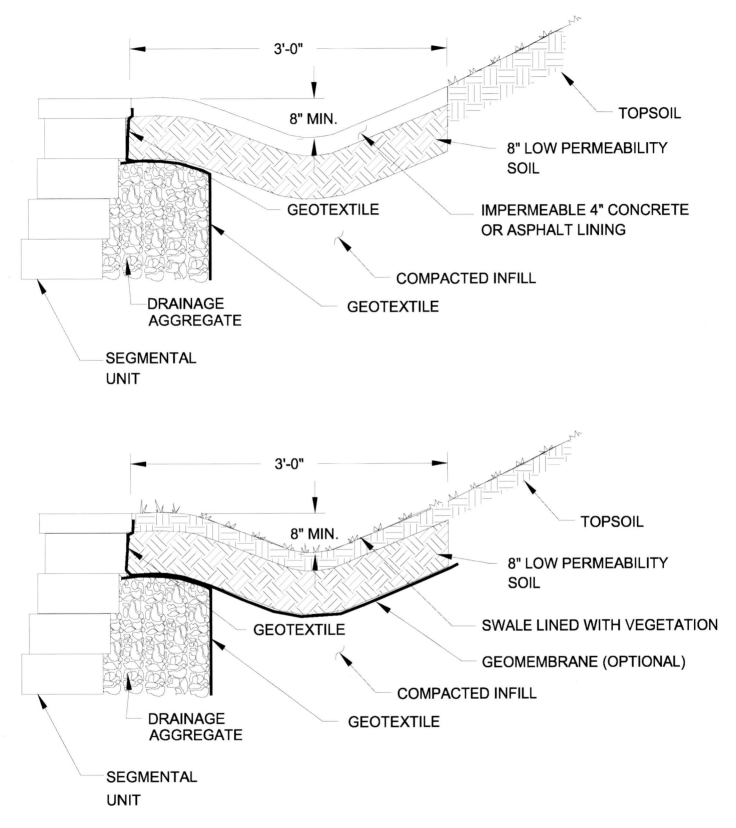

TOPSOIL

8" MIN.

8" LOW PERMEABILITY
SOIL

GEOTEXTILE

IMPERMEABLE 4" CONCRETE
OR ASPHALT LINING

COMPACTED INFILL

GEOTEXTILE

DRAINAGE
AGGREGATE

SEGMENTAL
UNIT

3'-0"

TOPSOIL

8" MIN.

8" LOW PERMEABILITY
SOIL

GEOTEXTILE

SWALE LINED WITH VEGETATION

GEOMEMBRANE (OPTIONAL)

COMPACTED INFILL

GEOTEXTILE

DRAINAGE
AGGREGATE

SEGMENTAL
UNIT

Figure 2 – Example Drainage Swale [Ref. 2]

It is often difficult, if not infeasible, to place a drainage swale at the top of a retaining wall. In many situations, soil slopes behind a retaining wall direct surface water flow towards the wall and overtop (Figure 3). If the water is not clean, there exists a potential for the water to stain the wall facing. One method for minimizing the potential for staining is to provide an overflow point that directs surface water over the wall without allowing the water to flow down the wall facing. A scupper is an overflow structure that accomplishes this goal. A scupper functions in much the same manner as the roof overhang on a home. Water flowing off the roof falls to the ground without flowing down the exterior face of the home, thus surface erosion and staining of the home's exterior face is minimized. Figure 4 illustrates a scupper constructed at the top of a segmental retaining wall.

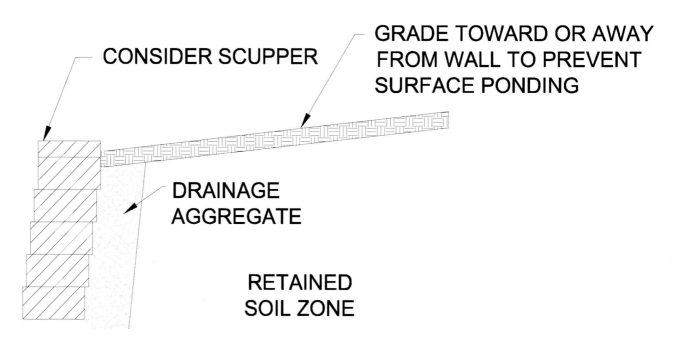

CONSIDER SCUPPER

GRADE TOWARD OR AWAY FROM WALL TO PREVENT SURFACE PONDING

DRAINAGE AGGREGATE

RETAINED SOIL ZONE

Figure 3 – Example of Grading without Drainage Swale [Ref. 2]

Figure 4 – Typical Scupper at top of Segmental Retaining Wall [Ref. 2]

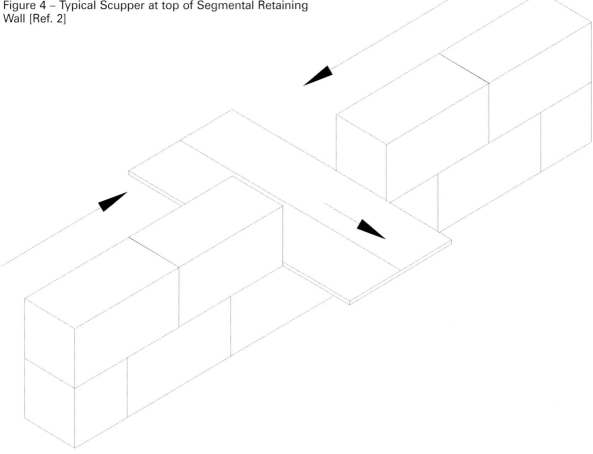

As illustrated in Figure 2, a geotextile filter fabric is placed as a separator between the low permeability soil, compacted fill, and drainage aggregate. It is important that the geotextile filter fully separate the low permeability soil from the drainage aggregate. This is often accomplished by extending the geotextile filter up the back of wall to the top of soil fill behind the wall or just below the finished grade. The geotextile filter will prevent the fine-grained, low permeability soil from piping (washing) into and through the drainage aggregate. When the geotextile filter is not present depressions, holes and settlement of the fill behind the wall can occur as the low permeability soil migrates into the drainage aggregate. Once in the drainage aggregate, the low permeability soil will reduce the drainage capacity of the drainage aggregate or wash through the aggregate and onto the wall facing. Backfill washing onto the wall facing often leads to poor wall aesthetics.

## Drainage

Drainage aggregate or transition fill is a component of a segmental retaining wall system. Depending on its function, the drainage aggregate provides several benefits:

• Prevent the build up of hydrostatic pressure behind the segmental retaining wall units, within the compacted backfill soil (retained soil in a gravity wall and reinforced fill in a soil reinforced wall) and foundation soils in close proximity of the bottom of wall.

• When properly designed, serves as a natural soil filter, preventing retained soils from washing through the face of the wall and staining the wall.

• Facilitates compaction of the fill directly behind the segmental retaining wall units.

Figure 5 illustrates an example wall section where geotextile filter fabric and drainage aggregate assist to minimize the buildup of hydrostatic pressure.

The ability for a soil to perform as a drainage aggregate is directly related to the its particle distribution or gradation, more specifically the percentage of soil particles passing the No. 200 sieve. In simplest terms, the soil must be free-draining, and a free-draining soil has less than 5 percent passing the No. 200 sieve and less than 7 percent passing the No. 100 sieve. Therefore, a soil that is considered coarse-grained is not necessarily free-draining.

When selecting a soil for use as a drainage aggregate (transition fill), the National Concrete Masonry Association recommends the soil meet the following particle gradation:

| Sieve Size | Percent Passing |
|------------|-----------------|
| 1 inch | 100 |
| 3/4 inch | 75-100 |
| No. 4 | 0-60 |
| No. 40 | 0-50 |
| No. 200 | 0-5 |

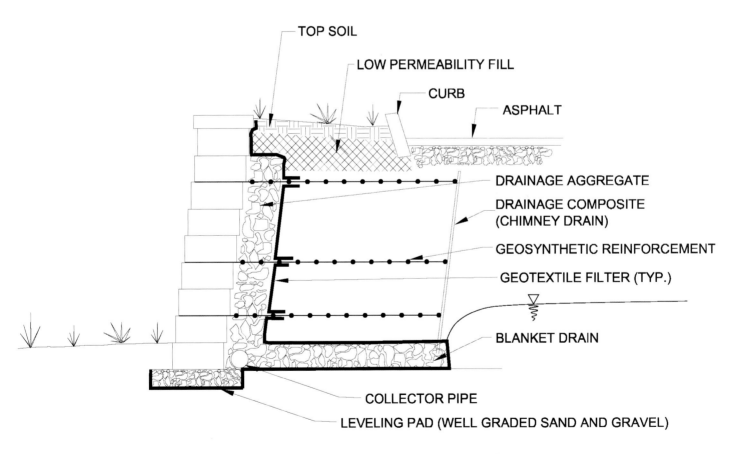

Figure 5 – Illustration of Geotextile Filter and Drainage Aggregate [Ref. 2]

Local quarries or landscape centers can assist in identify soils that meets this gradation. Many quarries utilize industry standard designations in defining aggregates available for construction. A clean or washed No. 67 stone will typically comply with the above recommendation.

Many soils will meet the referenced drainage aggregate gradation, but not every material will work as a natural soil filter. The soil filter must not only prevent the fines from adjacent soil from washing through, but it must also remain free-draining. The design techniques for evaluating filter characteristics of a soil require the gradation of the proposed drainage aggregate and the gradation of the soil it is to filter. The gradation of the drainage aggregate is often readily available from aggregate distributors; however, the gradation of the soil to be filtered often requires a gradation analysis.

When a soil can not function as a natural filter, a geotextile filter can be used to prevent the migration of fines from adjacent soils into the drainage aggregate. Geotextile filter design requires the gradation of the drainage aggregate and the apparent opening size (AOS) of the geotextile to be defined.

In selecting sources of drainage aggregate or appropriate geotextile filter fabric, it is advised that one coordinate with local experts for proper material selection. Local resources include landscape centers, landscape design firms, transportation departments, geosynthetic suppliers, segmental retaining wall system suppliers, and geotechnical engineering firms.

The drainage aggregate also provides a structural or construction benefit. A zone of drainage aggregate placed directly behind the segmental retaining wall units will facilitate compaction of the adjacent soils. Segmental retaining wall construction involves the compaction of the drainage aggregate, reinforced fill, retained soils and other soil placed as part of the wall erection.

## Compaction

The ability to compact a soil is a function of the type of soil, thickness of soil layer being compacted and moisture content (amount of water in the soil) of the soil. All soils have a unique relationship between their moisture content and maximum density. This relationship is known as a moisture-density relationship. It is different for every soil and is determined through laboratory testing. ASTM D698, *Moisture Density Relationship of Soils, Standard Method* (Standard Proctor Density) is one test method for determining a soil's unique moisture-density relationship. Using ASTM D698, curves similar to that shown in Figure 6 can be developed.

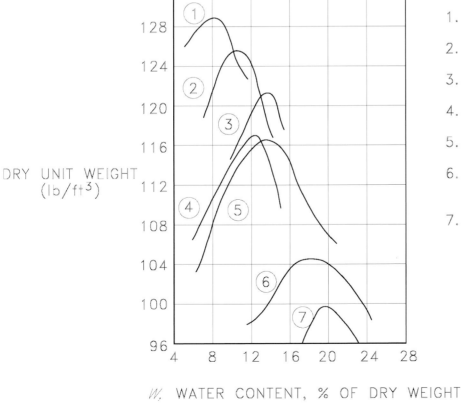

1. WELL GRADED COARSE TO FINE SAND. DENVER, COLO.
2. VERY FINE SILTY SAND. DENVER, COLO.
3. OXIDIZED CLAY TILL. CHICAGO, ILL.
4. CLAYEY SAND. CLINTON, MISS.
5. GLACIAL CLAY TILL. CHAMPAIGN, ILL.
6. OHIO RIVER FLOOD-PLAIN SILT. CINCINNATI, OHIO
7. SANDY SILT. WALLULA GAP, WASH.

Figure 6 – Typical Moisture-Density Relationship [Ref.1]

Once a moisture-density relationship is established for a soil, the water content corresponding to the maximum dry unit weight of the soil is defined. This water content is defined as the optimum water content. An engineer can then specify that a soil be placed and compacted at a moisture content close to or equal to the optimum moisture content. The engineer will then be assured the soil placed and compacted in the field achieves the density assumed during design. This is important to define in that the design and performance of a segmental retaining wall is a direct function of the shear strength of the soil. The shear strength of soil is directly related to the compacted density of the soil.

Soil compaction is commonly achieved by three methods; 1) Vibration, 2) Ramming, or 3) Static load. Vibration involves shaking of the soil particles in close proximity of the compaction equipment resulting in rearranging of the soil particles and increased soil density. Ramming is similar to vibration in that the soil particles are rearranged and densified, except the equipment utilizes lower frequencies and greater amplitude to achieved compaction. Ramming breaks down the soil and forces air out by pushing soil particles closer together. Static compaction equipment uses only its self-weight and is best for very thin soil layers. Static compaction is usually used on asphalt. An additional difference between vibration and ramming is the amount of energy imparted to the soil during compaction operations. Ramming equipment is more often used on fine-grained soils (clay) that require greater effort to achieve desired compaction. [Ref. 14]

If a specific soil density must be achieved to ensure structural performance and that density is a function of how much it is compacted, then it is apparent that a soil easy to compact is beneficial. Drainage aggregate as defined in this book is easy to compact and is not greatly influenced by moisture content. By placing a zone of drainage aggregate directly behind the segmental retaining wall, less energy is required to compact the soil, and the potential for the segmental retaining wall unit to move during compaction is minimized.

Local wall contractors will be familiar with local soils and will be able to properly select appropriate equipment to build segmental retaining walls. Within the range of soils recommended by NCMA for segmental retaining wall construction, a vibratory plate compactor has proven safe and effective when compacting the drainage aggregate and soil within three feet of the segmental retaining wall units.

# Geosynthetics

Geosynthetics are manufactured materials made from synthetics or polymers with specific material properties. They are used in a wide range of products including high-strength ropes and straps, clothing, home furnishings, and construction materials. In construction, geosynthetics have made themselves useful in many different forms [Ref. 8.]:

- Geotextiles - reinforcement and filters
- Geogrids - reinforcement
- Geonets - drainage
- Geomembranes - containment
- Geopipe - buried plastic pipe
- Geosynthetic Clay Liners - landfill liners
- Geocomposites - products consisting of some combination of geotextile, geogrid, geonet, or geomembrane

Geotextiles and geogrids are the two most common geosynthetic materials used in segmental retaining wall construction. Geopipe and geocomposites represent another group of geosynthetics used in conjunction with segmental retaining wall construction. Geotextiles and geogrids often serve a similar function when used as soil reinforcement. Geotextiles are also used as separators or filter fabrics.

Geotextiles consist of synthetic fibers, not natural fibers such as cotton, wool, or silk as found in traditional textiles, and geotextiles represent one of the two largest groups of geosynthetics. Example synthetic fibers include polyester and polypropylene, which are both resistant to a broad range of chemical and biological attack. Thus biodegradation is usually not a problem. Geotextiles are manufactured into flexible, porous fabric by weaving machinery or matted together in a random, non-woven pattern. Since geotextiles are porous they allow water to flow across or through the geotextile, or within like a conduit. Numerous applications exist for geotextiles; however, the following is a list of several discrete functions [Ref. 8]:

- Separation
- Reinforcement
- Filtration
- Drainage

Geogrids are plastics or synthetic fibers formed into very open grid-like structures. Geogrids are made by stretching sheet drawn material in one or two directions, or made by weaving strands into an open grid pattern. Geogrids are made from polyester, polypropylene, polyethylene or other structural synthetic materials. Geogrids differ from geotextile tile in that they have larger open areas that allow them to more efficiently interface with soil. Geogrids are used most often as a reinforcement element [Ref. 8].

Geosynthetic materials (geogrids and

geotextiles) used in segmental retaining walls will often be specified to meet minimum specified material properties. Geotextiles are specified based on material properties such as apparent open area (critical parameter for water flow and filtration), puncture strength, tear strength, and water flow rate. Geogrid and geotextile soil reinforcements are often required to meet specific material properties such as allowable reinforcement tension, pullout interaction coefficient, and direct sliding coefficient. Each parameter plays an important part in the design and performance of a segmental retaining wall.

## Geotextiles Filter

Minimum material properties ensure that the geotextile filter will perform as intended. The apparent opening size (AOS) is defined as the U.S. standard sieve number that has openings closest in size to the openings in the filter. An AOS of 40 implies the geotextile openings are equivalent to that of the No. 40 U.S. sieve. The No. 40 U.S. sieve is a mesh screen with square openings equal to 0.420 mm. The AOS is used in quantifying the filter characteristics of the geotextile filter and is used in evaluating the compatibility of a geotextile filter with the soil it is intended to retain. Puncture strength and tear strength ensures the geotextile has sufficient durability and survivability for the intended appli-

cations. Since the geotextile is often placed between the drainage aggregate and retained soil during compaction, the geotextile must have sufficient strength to ensure the aggregate does not puncture or tear the geotextile. Holes in the geotextile will alter the filter and drainage characteristics of the material. Water flow rate is a very important parameter in selecting geotextile materials. There are many available geotextile products that satisfy filter and strength requirements, but these materials will have varying water flow rates. The purpose of the geotextile filter is to allow water to pass through while preventing soil fines from passing. The water flow rate of the geotextile filter needs to be greater than or equal to the flow rate of the water flowing through the system. Otherwise, the geotextile filter will restrict the flow of water within the soil causing the water to backup. This leads to the development of hydrostatic pressure, which is an undesired loading condition in retaining wall applications.

## Geogrid and Geotextile Soil Reinforcement

Geogrid and Geotextile soil reinforcements are the structural element in reinforced soil retaining walls. The soil reinforcement interacts with the compacted soil fill to create a composite soil mass. This composite soil mass provides stability to the segmental retaining wall.

*Courtesy of Rockwood Retaining Walls*

Within the composite soil mass, the soil reinforcement must be sized and selected to prevent rupture of the reinforcement, slippage of the reinforcement within the soil, slippage or rupture of the reinforcement at the segmental retaining wall unit interface, and sliding. Geometry, load and soil properties dictate reinforcement type and length. Many soil reinforcement products are available for segmental retaining wall construction, and many can be directly substituted for one another, but not all. Figure 7 illustrates the various design issues addressed with soil reinforcement.

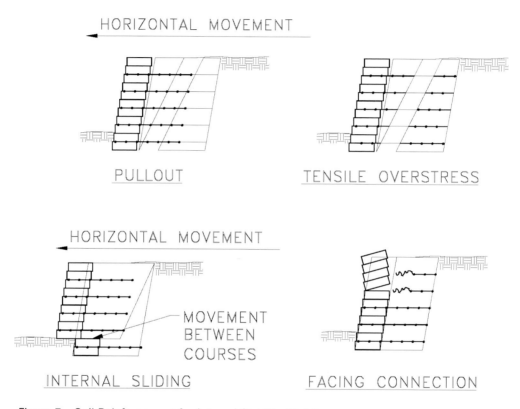

Figure 7 – Soil Reinforcement for Internal Stability [Ref.1]

Allowable reinforcement tension ensures the soil reinforcement will not rupture within the composite mass or at the geosynthetic and segmental retaining wall unit interface. The pullout interaction coefficient defines the degree to which the reinforcement can resist being pulled out of the soil. It is a measure of efficiency, and not all soil reinforcements have the same interaction coefficient. The lower the coefficient, the longer the required reinforcement length to resist pullout. The direct sliding coefficient is a measure of the reinforcement interaction with a soil sliding across. The higher the direct sliding coefficient the lessor the influence the reinforcement has on the sliding resistance of the soil. The facing connection capacities of segmental retaining wall systems are not equal. Each wall system and geosynthetic soil reinforcement combination will have specific facing connection capacity.

It is important that the system supplier or wall designer be consulted whenever a material substitution is made to ensure all performance impacts are evaluated. When constructing segmental retaining walls in accordance with the system supplier's recommendation, it is important to utilize the specified materials to ensure the long-term performance of the wall.

# Chapter 3
# Segmental Retaining Wall Maintenance and Aesthetics

## Maintenance and Cleaning

### Maintenance

Segmental retaining wall units are durable, flexible, and economic concrete products that provide high quality architecturally and aesthetically pleasing solutions to retaining wall applications. Segmental retaining wall units are manufactured to perform over the life of the structure and generally require little to no maintenance to maintain aesthetic quality.

In many cases, basic maintenance steps can be employed that will ensure the longevity of the segmental retaining wall units. The simplest of these steps is periodic assessment of the units or the segmental retaining wall's condition. While the majority of the inspection can be done by visual assessment, inspection and maintenance of subsurface drainage and drainage outlet pipes may require more than visual inspection. Table 2 is a simple list of regular inspections and frequency that can be conducted on segmental retaining walls.

### Cleaning

Periodic cleaning of segmental retaining walls may be needed to remove dirt, stains, efflorescence, graffiti, or mold. A wide range of resources are available to the public regarding the cleaning of masonry, including concrete masonry suppliers, landscape installers, segmental retaining wall system suppliers and industry associations. The National Concrete Masonry Association maintains publications addressing the cleaning of masonry. NCMA TEK 8-2A, *Removal of Stains from Concrete Masonry* provides information on removing a wide range of stains and NCMA TEK 8-3A, *Control and Removal of Efflorescence* discusses control and removal of efflorescence. Both NCMA documents are appropriate when evaluating cleaning options for segmental retaining wall units.

As a general rule with any cleaning effort, care should be taken to use the least aggressive approach so as not to damage the concrete masonry unit or adversely alter the unit's aesthetics. Recommendations from the cleaning agent's manufacturer should be closely adhered to since some products can alter the unit or cause serious personal injury.

Prior to any cleaning effort, the source of the stain should be identified and remedied if possible so that future cleaning can be avoided. Cleaning should start in a small inconspicuous area so the effect of cleaning can be evaluated without impacting the entire segmental retaining wall. Once the effectiveness of the cleaning method is evaluated it can be applied to the entire segmental retaining wall.

### MAINTENANCE SCHEDULE [REF. 13]

| Inspection | Frequency |
|---|---|
| Check the overall appearance of the structure for any signs of damage or poor performance. | Periodically |
| Check vertical and horizontal alignment of wall surfaces. | Every 2 to 5 years |
| Check for the presence of dirt, efflorescence and graffiti. Clean as necessary. | Annually |
| Examine drainage outlets to ensure proper function. | Bi-annually |
| Check for locations and sources of water. | Annually (Spring) |
| Examine condition of coatings, if any | Annually |
| Examine the condition of cap units and effectiveness of cap unit adhesive. | Annually |
| Check to make sure roof drains, downspouts or other water sources are directed away from wall or water collection structures are operating properly. Clean and repair as necessary. | Spring and Fall |
| Check to make sure grade slopes away from wall or drainage structures (swales) are working properly. | Annually (Spring) |
| Check presence of large trees and shrubs, evaluate impact of root structure. | Annually |
| Check drainage outlets for presence of vermin. Remove nests and clean out as necessary. Install vermin caps or screens on outlet pipes, as necessary. | Annually |

# Vegetation - Selection and Placement

The flexibility and range of products available for constructing segmental retaining walls makes them ideal for landscape projects. Segmental retaining walls are easy to install systems that create grade separation, creating a multitude of ground areas where plantings can be placed to create visually stunning landscapes. When selecting vegetation, whether it is flowers, grass, low-growth plantings, shrubs, or trees, it is important to understand how plantings will interact with the segmental retaining wall. It is equally important to understand how the segmental retaining wall will interact with plantings and vegetation.

*Courtesy of ICD Corporation*

*Courtesy of Risi Stone Systems*

This is an example of a retaining wall which integrates both concrete block and foliage. *Courtesy of Kirchner Brick and Block, Inc.*

Retaining walls provide a natural background to floral gardens.
*Courtesy of Allan Block Corporation*

Segmental retaining walls are constructed using a wide range of soils, both granular (free or fast draining) and fine-grained (slow draining). All soils placed during construction of segmental retaining walls are placed in thin lifts (6 to 8 inches maximum) and compacted. Compacting soil is beneficial to structural performance, but compaction can have an adverse affect on a soil's ability to sustain vegetation. Balance between structural and agronomic needs is important to successfully sustain vegetation.

Compacting soil rearranges the soil particles; removes air voids; and increases soil density. Engineers specify compaction requirements to achieve desired engineering properties for the soil, such as shear strength and erodibility. Vegetation performs best in soils that have sufficient interconnected void space (channels within the soil), which allows storage and passage of air and water in the soil. Vegetation requires some level of compaction to be achieved in the soil so large voids are closed and suitable density is achieved. It is generally recognized that high densities required by engineers for structural capacity tends to reduce or effectively stop the development of roots. Depending on the type of vegetation, soil compaction can restrict root growth, reduce root lengths, and prevent root penetration[Ref. 6].

Vegetation growth can be improved if the soil surface is modified after compaction and prior to planting. Modification includes furrowing, scarification, disking, ripping, or tracking. These methods and others open the top surface of compacted soil providing porous surfaces that are better for vegetation growth. It is important to recognize that these methods of modification often create soil surfaces that are more susceptible to erosion. The risk must be evaluated and appropriate erosion control measures introduced to minimize erosion (e.g. placing erosion control blankets or mulching over newly seeded surfaces) [Ref.7].

Trees interact with retaining walls in a variety of ways. Root growth within the soil mass behind the retaining wall will act like soil reinforcement, thus assist in stabilizing the structure. Depending on the location of the tree, extensive lateral root growth can result in root growth through the wall facing; however, in many cases the drainage aggregate and segmental retaining wall units will serve as a sufficient barrier to root growth. Roots require sufficient water and soil structure to grow. Drainage aggregate generally does not support root growth. Also depending on the location, the tree may exert lateral load on the segmental retaining wall system during wind events. Sufficient support must be present around the base of the tree to ensure it does not topple as a result of inadequate support. Local landscape centers or similar professional service centers can provide recommendations with tree plantings behind retaining walls. Keep in mind that root ball installation requires the excavated hole for the root ball to be 1.5 to 2.0 times greater in diameter than the rootball itself. Care should be taken to leave a zone of undisturbed soil behind the retaining wall, so initial lateral support can be provided or sufficient soil support is present for staking, until root growth is established. Again, follow the staking recommendations of your local landscape center.

*Courtesy of Risi Stone Systems*

Location of plantings relative to the location of the segmental retaining wall will impact the growth potential of that planting. North facing walls will cast a shadow on plantings placed at the wall's base. In addition to lighting considerations, plantings should be selected based on available water. Control of surface water will minimize the potential for flooding of vegetated areas. Again, it is important to consult local landscape centers for advice on plant selection and placement.

*Courtesy of Rockwood Retaining Walls*

*Courtesy of Pacific Precast Products*

## Plantings and Trenching – Interaction with Soil Reinforcement

The stability of a reinforced soil segmental retaining wall is depended upon the integrity of the geosynthetic soil reinforcement. If the reinforcement is damaged, cut, or removed, the integrity and stability of the segmental retaining wall may be jeopardized.

Care should be taken during the excavation for plantings, trenching for utilities, or irrigation systems. In the event the soil reinforcement is damaged, immediate repair should be made in accordance with the system supplier's recommendation. In some cases, new sections of soil reinforcement can be placed at the location of damage with minimal (typically 3 feet) overlap of in-place reinforcement. In other cases, the entire length of soil reinforcement may require exposing and replacing.

When constructing a reinforced soil segmental retaining wall, one should consider placing strips of warning tape or similar material above the uppermost layer of reinforcement. This can be accomplished by laying the material at regular intervals on the next level of compacted fill, and to the same lengths as the soil reinforcement. It is also advisable to minimize trenching operations within 3 feet of the reinforced soil segmental retaining wall. This assures some initial length of reinforcement is available during repair, in the event the reinforcement is cut during trenching operations. Reinforcement cut directly behind the segmental retaining wall unit requires deconstruction of the segmental retaining wall so proper connection can be reestablished between the soil reinforcement and wall units.

# Tiered, Multi-level Segmental Retaining Walls

*Courtesy of Allan Block Corporation*

The ease and flexibility of segmental retaining walls makes them ideal for constructing curved structures that conform to geometrical constraints. In addition to horizontal contouring, segmental retaining walls are easy to construct in multi-level configurations. Multi-leveled or tiered walls break up tall retaining structures and provide ideal landings for landscape features.

In some instances, the construction of a tiered retaining wall reduces the structural requirements of lower tiers, but this is not always the case. The structural requirements of lower levels are a func-

tion of the distance between successive tiers. Three scenarios are possible when evaluating tiered retaining walls:

1. The retaining walls are of sufficient distance apart that neither influences the stability of the other.
2. The retaining walls are sufficiently close that each wall will influence the structural requirements of the other.
3. The retaining walls are sufficiently close together that they function as a single retaining wall.

33

This multi-leveled retaining wall provides access to the backyard from different stories of the house. *Courtesy of Allan Block Corporation*

Terracing tames a hill. *Courtesy of Anchor Wall Systems*

Designers use sophisticated computer programs to calculate applied load when determining the influence of individual retaining wall tiers on each other. Through engineering analysis, designers can specify the size of segmental retaining wall units necessary in conventional gravity walls to ensure stability, or specify the number of layers, type, and length of soil reinforcement in reinforced soil segmental retaining walls. In addition to software, engineers use guidelines like those presented in Figure 8 to evaluate the impact of tiered structures.

As a basic rule for tiered walls, the National Concrete Masonry Association suggests the following:

1. If the total combined height of the tiered walls is less than 6 ft and the horizontal spacing between each tier is equal to or greater than 2 times the height of the lower wall, then the wall can be constructed and designed in accordance with the segmental retaining wall system supplier's design chart solutions.

2. If the horizontal spacing is less than twice the height of the lower wall, and the overall combined height is 6 ft or more, the proposed segmental retaining wall should be reviewed by a design professional. This is consistent with many local building codes that require permits or design review by a design professional for walls over 4 to 6 ft.

TO DETERMINE APPROXIMATE SURCHARGE
OF UPPER WALL 2 ON LOWER WALL 1
IMPLEMENT BY ITERATIVE PROCESS

1. ESTIMATE BASE LENGTH $L_1$, AND CALCULATE
   EXTERNAL FAILURE ANGLE,

2. CALCULATE $q_{\ell 1}$, AND $q_{d1}$, BASED UPON $L_1$

3. CALCULATE ACTUAL $L_1$ BASED UPON EXTERNAL
   STABILITY ANALYSIS USING $q_{\ell 1}$, AND $q_{d1}$,
   FROM STEP 2

4. IF CALCULATED $L_1$ (STEP 3) < ESTIMATED $L_1$
   (STEP 1). OK. IF NOT REPEAT STEPS 1–4

5. CHECK GLOBAL/OVERALL STABILITY OF
   FINAL GEOMETRIC CONFIGURATION

J = HORIZONTAL DISTANCE FROM
    WALL FACE TO WALL FACE

L = BASE LENGTH OF
    GEOSYNTHETIC REINFORCEMENT
    FOR SOIL REINFORCED SRWs
    AND BASE WIDTH OF
    CONVENTIONAL SRWs

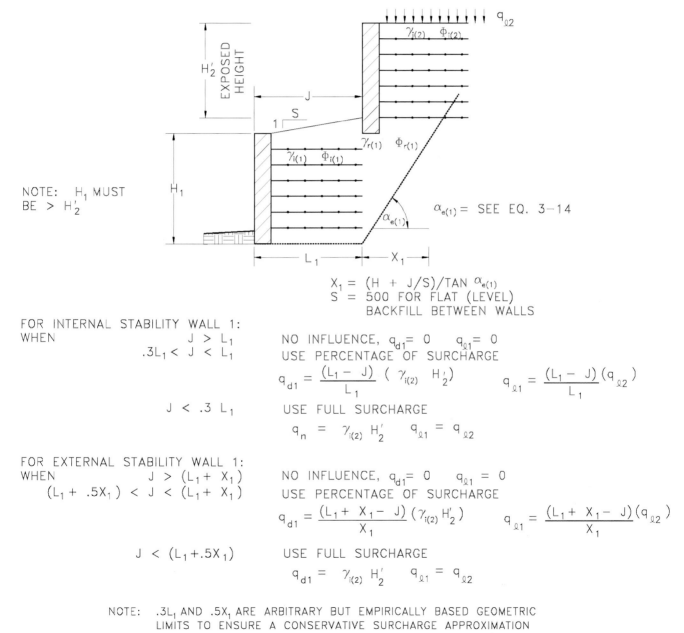

NOTE: $H_1$ MUST
BE > $H_2'$

$X_1 = (H + J/S)/TAN\ \alpha_{e(1)}$
$S = 500$ FOR FLAT (LEVEL)
     BACKFILL BETWEEN WALLS

FOR INTERNAL STABILITY WALL 1:
WHEN $\qquad J > L_1 \qquad$ NO INFLUENCE, $q_{d1}= 0 \qquad q_{\ell 1}= 0$
$.3L_1 < J < L_1 \qquad$ USE PERCENTAGE OF SURCHARGE

$$q_{d1} = \frac{(L_1 - J)}{L_1}(\gamma_{i(2)}\ H_2') \qquad q_{\ell 1} = \frac{(L_1 - J)}{L_1}(q_{\ell 2})$$

$J < .3\ L_1 \qquad$ USE FULL SURCHARGE

$$q_n = \gamma_{i(2)}\ H_2' \qquad q_{\ell 1} = q_{\ell 2}$$

FOR EXTERNAL STABILITY WALL 1:
WHEN $\qquad J > (L_1 + X_1) \qquad$ NO INFLUENCE, $q_{d1}= 0 \qquad q_{\ell 1} = 0$
$(L_1 + .5X_1) < J < (L_1 + X_1) \qquad$ USE PERCENTAGE OF SURCHARGE

$$q_{d1} = \frac{(L_1 + X_1 - J)}{X_1}(\gamma_{i(2)}\ H_2') \qquad q_{\ell 1} = \frac{(L_1 + X_1 - J)}{X_1}(q_{\ell 2})$$

$J < (L_1 + .5X_1) \qquad$ USE FULL SURCHARGE

$$q_{d1} = \gamma_{i(2)}\ H_2' \qquad q_{\ell 1} = q_{\ell 2}$$

NOTE: $.3L_1$ AND $.5X_1$ ARE ARBITRARY BUT EMPIRICALLY BASED GEOMETRIC
LIMITS TO ENSURE A CONSERVATIVE SURCHARGE APPROXIMATION

Figure 8 – Tiered Wall Design Chart for Engineers [Ref. 1]

# Chapter 4
# Segmental Retaining Wall Construction

The success of any retaining wall installation depends on complete and accurate field information, careful planning and scheduling, the use of specified materials, proper construction procedures, and inspection during and after the construction process. This is true for the construction of both conventional gravity segmental retaining walls and reinforced soil segmental retaining walls. Regardless of the type of project, there are many simple steps that can be followed that ensure success, some of which are as follows:

Verify the wall location prior to and during construction operations.

Verify existing and proposed wall grade prior to construction to ensure actual constructed wall height agrees with the proposed wall height and material quantity estimates.

Coordinate delivery and storage of materials at the wall site to ensure unobstructed acess to the work area and availability of materials.

Ensure that any materials delivered to the wall site are accompanied by the manufacturer's certification or supplier's invoice so that correct materials are used during construction.

Ensure that damaged segmental retaining wall units or incorrect geosynthetic materials are rejected and the suppliers of the products notified immediately.

Always check with the local utility companies to be sure that digging does not interfere with, or damage, underground pipelines or conduits.

Check with local building codes or officials regarding requirements for retaining wall construction.

Review the segmental retaining wall system supplier's recommended installation and structural requirements.

If constructing a conventional gravity segmental retaining wall, verify that the proposed wall height or geometry does not exceed the structural limitations of the segmental retaining wall system.

Inspect any soil materials delivered for construction to ensure they comply with the project requirements.

If constructing a tiered or multi-leveled retaining wall, evaluate the minimum offset between walls to ensure it agrees with structural assumptions used in selecting or identifying acceptable segmental retaining wall systems.

Review and inspect all system and project components required for construction as necessary. Segmental retaining wall components include, but are not limited to (Figure 9):

- Foundation – exposed and prepared in accordance with recommended guidelines for the applicable segmental retaining wall, leveling pad, compacted reinforced fill (as required), drainage aggregate, and compacted retaining fill.
- Wall embedment – minimum required burial depth for the retaining wall.
- Drainage aggregate – free-draining granular soil placed behind, within or within and behind the segmental retaining wall unit.
- Reinforced fill (if required) – designated soil that will be placed and compacted in conjunction with soil reinforcement to create a composite soil mass.
- Surface drainage – identify and address sources of surface water that can influence the wall during and after construction. Grading away from the wall and drainage swales are often used to address surface water.
- Geosynthetic reinforcement (if required) – durable, high strength polymer products designed specifically for reinforcing soil. Type and length requirements should be verified prior to and during construction

• Segmental retaining wall unit – concrete units designed and manufactured to perform as facing for conventional gravity and soil reinforced retaining walls. Pins, connectors, clips, bars or other devices utilized by segmental retaining wall units to provide resistance against lateral sliding or provide methods of attaching soil reinforcement.

• Geotextile filter – geosynthetic product designed to function as a soil filter and drainage media.

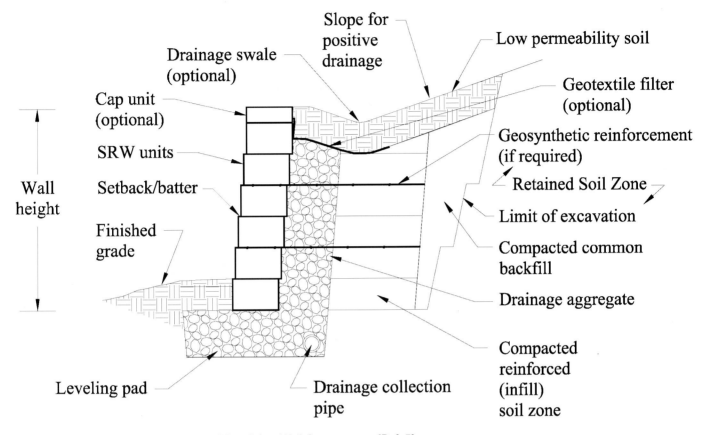

Figure 9 – Segmental Retaining Wall Components [Ref. 5]

## Planning

Proper planning will play a key role in ensuring that the checklist items provided above can be properly addressed. Proper planning will also assist in developing proper material estimates. Once the wall layout is established and structural considerations identified, local system suppliers can assist in quantifying the materials required for their individual systems. Many systems will require the addition of pins, connectors or similar components, or multiple block types that are used to create distinctive and attractive wall aesthetics.

It is important to consider minimum radii, wall setback, and areas needed for soil reinforcement when selecting a segmental retaining wall system. Each system is constructed to specific wall batter or setback. Wall setback will influence minimum constructed radii without needing to cut segmental retaining wall units. The setback will also influence wall layout as the top of the wall will not align directly with the base of the wall, and this needs consideration when abutting to other structures or evaluating minimum radii.

## Construction

Local system suppliers can assist in identifying necessary materials and tools required for the construction of their specific system. The following tools are generally useful in the construction of all segmental retaining wall systems:

- Concrete masonry unit splitter
- Diamond-blade concrete saw
- Safety protection equipment – including, but not limited to, goggles, gloves, ear plugs, dust masks, protective boots and other personal protection devices
- Vibratory plate compactor – verify compactor size with system supplier
- Hand tamper
- Masonry chisel – 3-inch
- Broom

- Shovel
- Brick/masonry hammer
- Sledge hammer
- Tape measure
- Caulking gun
- Backhoe or loader – as required by project size and complexity
- Four-foot level
- String line
- Layout/survey stakes
- Transit or site level

# Chapter Five

# Segmental Retaining Wall Construction (A Step-By-Step Guide)

[Ref. 5. (NCMA SRW Installation Guide, 2002)]

## Excavation

Excavate to the lines and grades required for proper installation of the segmental retaining wall. The installer should take precautions to minimize over-excavation and maintain safe slopes per OSHA requirements. There are two basic topographical conditions in which segmental retaining walls may be constructed; "cut" and "fill." The differences between the two are illustrated in Figure 10.

The construction approach, schedule, and cost will be dictated by the type of wall that is required at the site. Additionally, the effects of construction on existing nearby structures and parking areas must be carefully considered for "cut" walls such that the foundation support of those structures are not undermined or encroached upon in any way.

*Courtesy of Tensar Earth Technologies*

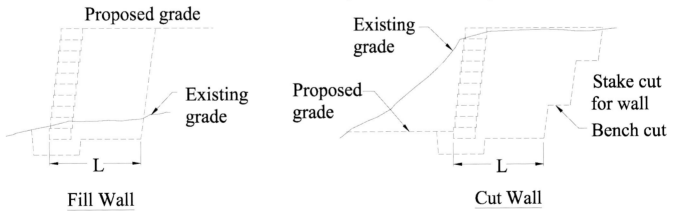

Fill Wall                    Cut Wall

**Wall Layout and General Excavation**

1. Survey stake SRW location and general excavation limits for wall construction.
2. Ensure SRW is along proper alignment, and within appropriate property boundaries, and construciton easements.
3. Perform general excavation for wall.

Figure 10 – Layout and Excavation

## Foundation Soil and Leveling Pad Construction

Foundation soil shall be excavated as required for base course leveling dimensions and limits of the reinforced soil zone. The foundation soils shall be examined to assure that it is adequate for supporting the proposed retaining wall structure. For walls less than 6 ft in total height, local experience or visual inspection may be sufficient. Otherwise, inspection by a professional is recommended.

Compact the foundation to required density per designer or system supplier's recommendations. If compaction requirements are not specified, the foundation soil should be compacted until no movement is observable with a passing of the compaction equipment. Material that can not be compacted or excessively loose, soft, wet or frozen should be removed and replaced with compacted granular fill.

The compacted soil leveling pad should be 6 inches minimum in thickness and constructed using GP, GW, SP or SW soil types, as identified in Table 1, for optimum stress distribution and drainage. The leveling pad should be densely compacted. Caution should be exercised in leveling the drainage aggregate to ensure intimate contact between the units and aggregate. Alternately, thin/weak concrete leveling courses may be poured above the compacted leveling pad to speed construction. The leveling pad should be no less than 6 inches from the toe and heel of the lowermost segmental retaining wall unit. See Figure 11.

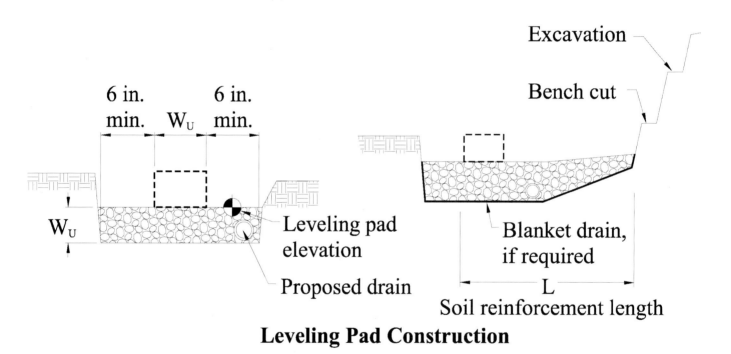

**Leveling Pad Construction**

1. Stake wall location for leveling pad excavation.
2. Excavate trench to create a minimum leveling pad thickness of 6 inches (152 mm) and to the minimum width shown.
3. Install drain pipe with positive gravity flow to outlet.
4. Place, level and compact leveling pad material for SRW units.
5. Place and compact aggregate blanket drain, install geotextile if required.

Figure 11 – Leveling Pad Construction

*Courtesy of Tensar
Earth Technologies*

*Courtesy of Allan
Block Corporation*

## Drainage Pipe Installation

Where applicable, a drainage pipe should be installed for most walls exceeding 3 ft. The drainage pipe assists in removing water from behind the segmental retaining wall. If no positive means for removing the water is available, such as directing collected water into existing storm water systems or onto downhill slopes in front of the wall, do not place pipes below lowest exposed segmental retaining wall unit. Provide outlets through the wall facing just above ground level. If no outlet is provided, water will collect and saturate the foundation soil jeopardizing the stability of the structure.

Consult with local system suppliers for appropriate drainage pipe materials. Some acceptable drainage pipe standards include: ASTM D3034, *Specification for Polyvinyl Chloride (PVC) Plastic Pipe* or ASTM D1248, *Specification for Corrugated Plastic Pipe*. The pipe may be covered with a geotextile sock to function as a filter. The drainage collection pipe shall be installed to maintain gravity flow of water to outside of the reinforced soil zone.

The drainage collection pipe should daylight into a storm sewer manhole or to a sloped area lower than the pipes behind the walls. The main collection drainpipe just behind the block facing shall be a minimum of 3 inches in diameter. The secondary collection drain pipes can function independently or tie into the main collection drain pipe with laterals at a nominal 50 foot spacing along the wall face. Do not place collector pipes below finished grade (at base of wall) if no means for outlet is provided. See Figure 11.

## Setting, Leveling, and Backfilling the First Course of SRW Units

All segmental retaining wall units shall be installed at proper elevation and orientation as recommended by the system supplier. The segmental retaining wall units shall be installed in general accordance with the manufacturer's recommendations. The completed wall erection shall be with $\pm$ 1.25 inches, measured over a 10 foot distance, in either a horizontal or vertical direction compared to the design line and grade control.

The first course of segmental retaining wall units shall be placed on the leveling pad. The units shall be checked for level and alignment. The first course is the most important to insure accurate and acceptable results. The installer should insure that the units are in full contact with the base. Units are placed side by side for the full length of the wall. Alignment may be done by means of a string line or offset from the base line to a molded finished face of the segmental retaining wall unit. Adjust unit spacing for curved sections according to the manufacturer's recommendations. See Figure 12.

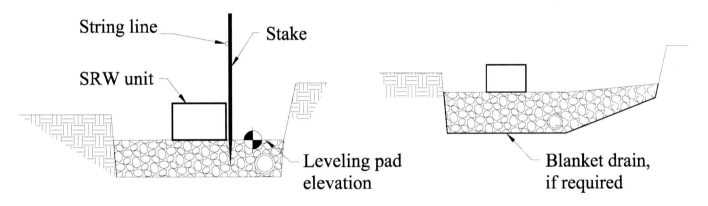

## Setting First Course of SRW Units

1. Check leveling pad elevation and smooth leveling pad surface.
2. Stake and stringline the wall location, pay close attention to exact location of curves, corners, vertical and horizontal steps. String line must be along a molded face of the SRW unit, and not along a broken block finish surface.
3. Install first course of SRW units, check level as placed.

Figure 12 – First Course Placement

Use drainage aggregate to fill any openings in and between segmental retaining wall units as required. The drainage aggregate shall be a clean 1-inch minus crushed stone or granular fill meeting the gradation discussed in Chapter 2.

The drainage aggregate shall be placed to a minimum thickness of 12 inches measured from the back of the segmental retaining wall unit, or as otherwise recommended by the system supplier. Carefully place drainage aggregate behind and up to the height of the segmental retaining wall unit to create the wall face drain. Install geotextile filter, if required.

In selecting a geotextile filter, woven or non-woven fabric with AOS of 70 - 100, minimum grab tensile strength of 110 pounds, and a minimum weight of 4 ounces/yard$^2$ is suggested. Or, consult with the system supplier.

The infill soil shall be placed behind the drainage aggregate as shown in the construction plans in 6-inch to 8-inch compacted lifts. Only hand operated compaction equipment (lightweight vibratory plate) should be allowed within 3 feet of the back of wall face. Place fill soil in front of the segmental retaining wall units. Compact the drainage and infill soil. See Figure 13.

Additional layers are installed, and backfill is added to aid in compaction. *Courtesy of Keystone Retaining Wall Systems, Inc.*

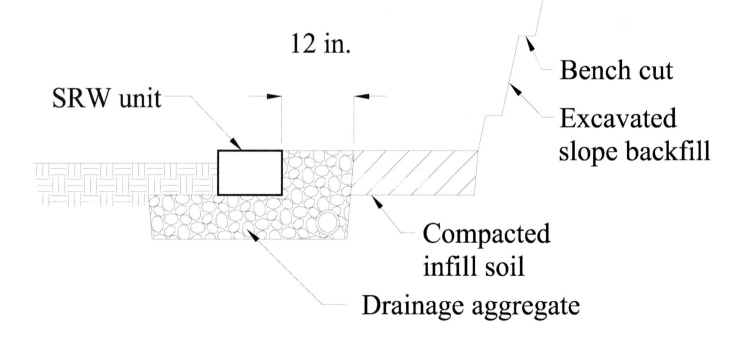

## Backfilling First Course of SRW Units

Figure 13 – First Course Backfilling

# Installing Successive Courses of SRWs

Ensure drainage aggregate is level with or slightly below the top of the segmental retaining wall unit below. Clean all debris off top of unit. Place and move segmental retaining wall unit to connectors, pins, clips or concrete lips and establish proper setback, consistent with manufacturer's recommendations. Check alignment and level of units and adjust as needed. See Figure 14.

Place drainage aggregate and infill soil as stated previously and per the manufacturer's specifications. See Figure 15.

*Courtesy of Tensar Earth Technologies*

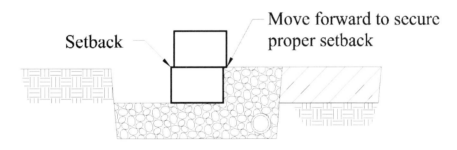

## Installing Successive Courses of SRW Units

1. Ensure the drainage aggregate is level with, or slightly below the top of SRW unit below.
2. Clean debris off top of unit.
3. Place SRW unit shear connectors if applicable.
4. Move SRW unit to engage shear connectors and establish proper setback, consistent with manufacturer's recommendations.

Figure 14 – Installing Successive Courses

*Courtesy of Allan Block Corporation*

## Placement and Tensioning of Reinforcement and Placement of Backfill

When segmental retaining walls require reinforcement, it is normally required on multiple levels extending from the face of the wall back into the compacted reinforced soil mass.

The soil reinforcement shall be installed at the proper elevation and orientation as shown in the approved construction plans, as directed by the engineer, or the manufacturer's recommendations.

Figure 15 – Fill Placement and Compaction

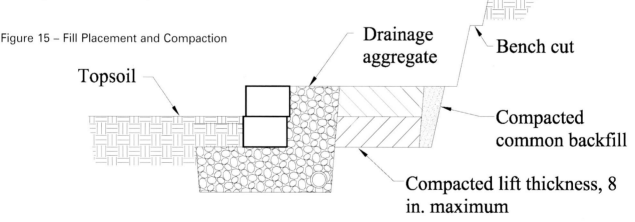

**Fill Placement and Compaction**

1. Use drainage aggregate to fill openings in and between SRW units, as required.
2. Place drainage aggregate behind and up to height of SRW unit to continue wall face drain. Install geotextile, if required.
3. Place and compact infill soil behind wall drain.
4. Compact drainage aggregate and infill soil.

Cut geosynthetic reinforcement to design length L as shown on the plans and install with design strength direction perpendicular to the wall face. The design strength direction is that length of geosynthetic reinforcement perpendicular to the wall face and shall be one continuous piece of material. Seams or overlaps of geosynthetic reinforcement parallel to the wall face are not permitted. Adjacent sections shall be butted in a manner to assure 100% coverage after placement.

Geosynthetic reinforcement should be installed under nominal tension. Apply a nominal tension to the reinforcement and maintain it by staples, stakes or hand tensioning. The tension applied may be released after the geosynthetic reinforcement has been covered and held in place with soil fill. See Figure 16.

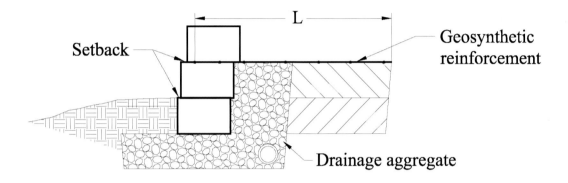

**Placement of Geosynthetic Reinforcement**

1. Ensure the drainage aggregate is level with, or slightly above the top of SRW unit below.
2. Clean debris off top of unit.
3. Cut geosynthetic reinforcement to design length L as shown on plans and install with strength direction perpendicular to wall face.
4. Place shear connectors, if applicable, as recommended by the manufacturer.
5. Place SRW unit on top of geosynthetic.
6. Move SRW unit to engage shear connectors and establish proper setback.

Figure 16 – Soil Reinforcement Placement

*Courtesy of Allan Block Corporation*

*Courtesy of Allan Block Corporation*

Place drainage aggregate for wall face drain in and between segmental retaining wall units as required by the specifications stated previously in this guide.

The reinforced soil zone shall be placed as shown in construction plans in 6-inch to 8-inch lifts and compacted. Soil shall be placed, spread and compacted in such a manner that eliminates the development of wrinkles and/or movement of the geosynthetic reinforcement. Only hand operated equipment should be allowed within 3 feet of the back of the wall units. Compact drainage aggregate following compaction of infill soil. See Figure 17.

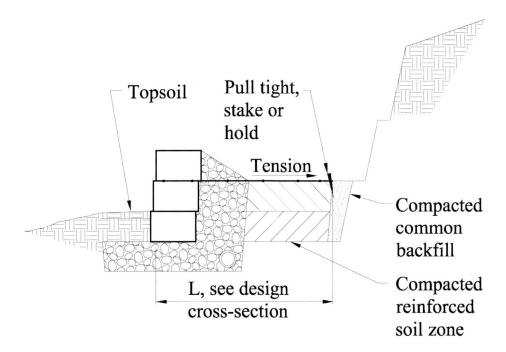

**Backfilling Over Geosynthetic Reinforcement**

1.  Sequence of backfilling steps may vary and are dependent on type of SRW unit and geosynthetic reinforcement used.
2.  Alignment of straight walls should be checked every other course.

Figure 17 – Backfill over Geosynthetic Reinforcement

Construction equipment shall not be operated directly on the geosynthetic reinforcement. A minimum backfill thickness of 6 inches is required prior to operation of vehicles over the geosynthetic reinforcement. Turning of vehicles should be kept to a minimum to prevent displacing the fill and damaging the geosynthetic reinforcement. Sudden breaking and sharp turning should be avoided.

For guidelines in placing geosynthetic soil reinforcement at corners and curves see Figures 18 and 19.

*Photo by Alexander Patho Photography*

Both squared edges and curves incorporated in the same retaining wall add some eye-catching charm. *Courtesy of R.I. Lampus Co.*

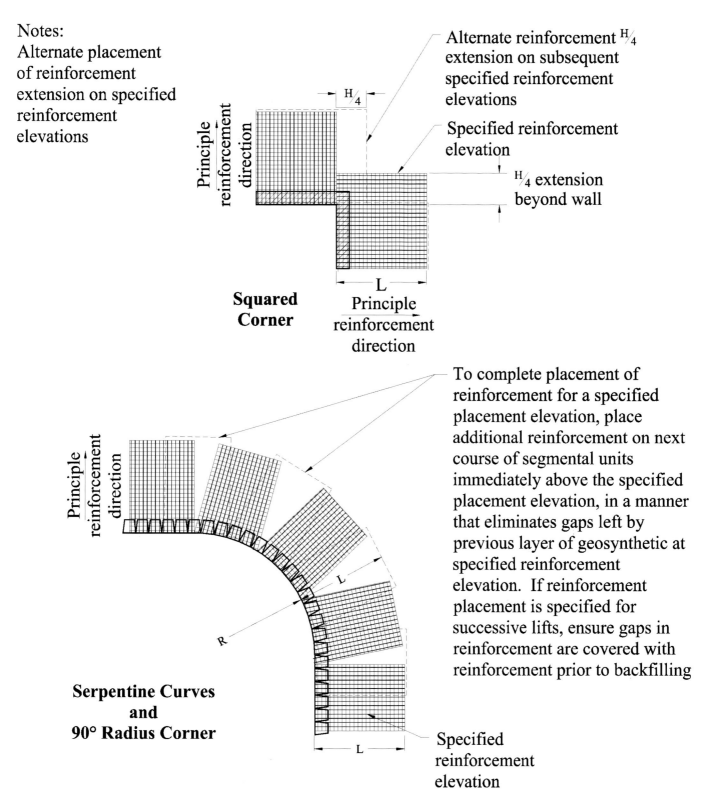

Notes:
Alternate placement of reinforcement extension on specified reinforcement elevations

Alternate reinforcement $H/4$ extension on subsequent specified reinforcement elevations

Specified reinforcement elevation

$H/4$ extension beyond wall

Principle reinforcement direction

**Squared Corner**

Principle reinforcement direction

To complete placement of reinforcement for a specified placement elevation, place additional reinforcement on next course of segmental units immediately above the specified placement elevation, in a manner that eliminates gaps left by previous layer of geosynthetic at specified reinforcement elevation. If reinforcement placement is specified for successive lifts, ensure gaps in reinforcement are covered with reinforcement prior to backfilling

Principle reinforcement direction

**Serpentine Curves and 90° Radius Corner**

Specified reinforcement elevation

Figure 18 – Reinforcement Placement for Concave Corners

Attractive curves and gentle shades of yellow and pink flowers soften this looming wall.
*Courtesy of Allan Block Corporation*

3 in. of soil required between overlapping reinforcement for proper anchorage if both layers placed at the same SRW unit elvation.

Alternative to overlapping in a single course, reinforcement could be placed in the perpendicular principle direction in the cross-over area on the succeeding course.

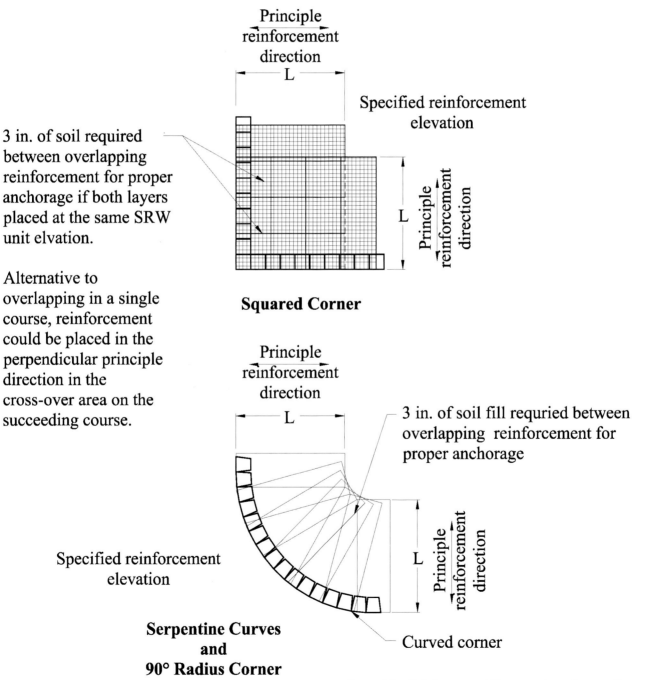

Principle reinforcement direction

L

Specified reinforcement elevation

L

Principle reinforcement direction

**Squared Corner**

Principle reinforcement direction

L

3 in. of soil fill requried between overlapping reinforcement for proper anchorage

Specified reinforcement elevation

L

Principle reinforcement direction

Curved corner

**Serpentine Curves
and
90° Radius Corner**

Figure 19 – Reinforcement Placement on Convex Corners

# Capping and Finish Grading

Install segmental retaining wall cap/coping unit (optional) and secure per manufacturer's recommendations.

Finished grade at the top and bottom of the wall and provide for positive drainage of water away from the segmental retaining wall system. Where the backfill above the wall slopes to the wall face, provide a drainage swale to collect direct runoff from flowing over the face of the system.

Provide a minimum of 1-foot low permeable soil to cap to the segmental retaining wall system to minimize infiltration of surface water into the soil. After topsoil placement, vegetate slopes above and around wall terminations. See Figure 20.

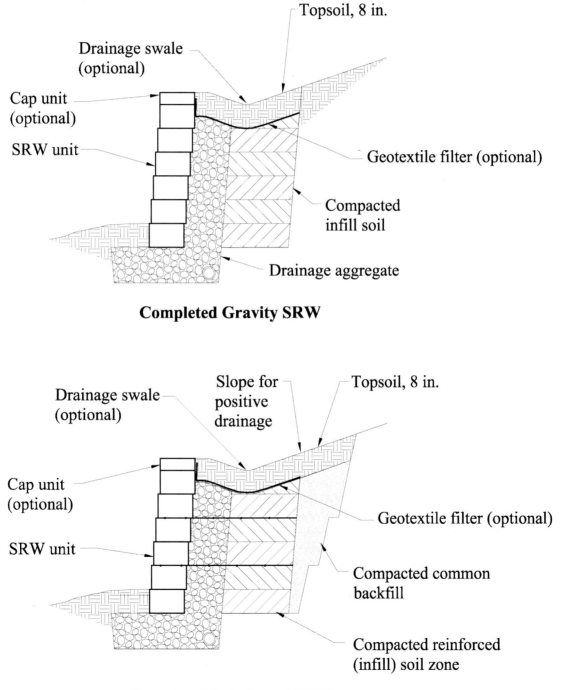

**Completed Gravity SRW**

**Completed Reinforced SRW**

Figure 20 – Complete Wall Sections

After cleaning off the last layer, a capstone is added as a finished touch. The cap may be flush or overhanging as required by aesthetics and design. *Courtesy of Keystone Retaining Wall Systems, Inc.*

*Courtesy of Allan Block Corporation*

*Photo by Alexander Patho Photography*

*Courtesy of R.I. Lampus Co.*

# Chapter 6
# Image Gallery

Retaining walls are perfect for creating a striking terraced hillside.
*Courtesy of Allan Block Corporation*

*Photo by Alexander Patho Photography*

*Courtesy of R.I. Lampus Co.*

Mulch, gravel, and other colorful materials are used to fill the planting beds within a multi-tiered wall to add style and variety. *Courtesy of Anchor Wall Systems.*

*Courtesy of Versa-Lok*

Retaining walls often have multiple terraces, which add planting space and definition to a hillside. *Courtesy of Versa-Lok*

Multi-colored and textured units can combine in a retaining wall to make a unique landscaping tool.
*Courtesy of Verşa-Lok*

A gradient retaining wall shores up a hillside and supports a driveway.
*Courtesy of Keystone Retaining Wall Systems, Inc.*

*Courtesy of Keystone Retaining Wall Systems, Inc.*

A series of wavy retaining walls provides an inviting backyard environ-
ment for this magnificent home. *Courtesy of Innovative Concrete Design*

Redefining the slope by maximizing land space, a series of retaining
walls add curb appeal to a front yard. *Courtesy of Anchor Wall Systems*

A small protrusion built onto the side of this retaining wall not only adds a place to plant, but a place to plant oneself! *Courtesy of Tensar Earth Technologies*

Tiered retaining walls create terraces, which split up a large grassy yard. *Courtesy of Tensar Earth Technologies*

Retaining walls built in front of residences add style and flair to an otherwise ordinary yard.
*Courtesy of Wilson Concrete Products*

*Photo by Alexander Patho Photography*

Retaining walls are used to define a backyard and to support a walkway around a private pond.
*Courtesy of R.I. Lampus Co.*

*Photo by Alexander Patho Photography*

Circular retaining walls serve as excellent planting areas.
*Courtesy of R.I. Lampus Co.*

Photo by Alexander Patho Photography

Curved retaining walls add form and depth to an expansive front yard.
*Courtesy of R.I. Lampus Co.*

Retaining walls often serve as foundations
for raised driveways, patios, and even pools.
*Courtesy of Risi Stone Systems*

*Courtesy of Versa-Lok*

A very popular and marketable feature of retaining walls is the option of units with lights, or even stereo equipment, built in. *Courtesy of Versa-Lok*

When creatively landscaped, an otherwise unexciting wall can turn into a beautiful backdrop for entertaining. *Courtesy of Wilson Concrete Products*

*Right:*
Rows of shrubs, flowers, and plants decorate the tiers of this protective retaining wall. *Courtesy of Risi Stone Systems*

Amidst these colorful retaining walls, one can sit peacefully and enjoy the landscaping. *Courtesy of Wilson Concrete Products*

This retaining wall follows the contour of the slightly modified natural stream beyond. *Courtesy of Anchor Wall Systems*

*Courtesy of Keystone Retaining Wall Systems, Inc.*

Water features can be incorporated into retaining walls to add a little flair. *Courtesy of Keystone Retaining Wall Systems, Inc.*

Retaining walls improve and reinforce vast hillsides. *Courtesy of Keystone Retaining Wall Systems, Inc.*

Shrubs become sculptural accents to a multi-tiered wall.
*Courtesy of Allan Block Corporation*

*Photo by Alexander Patho Photography*

A stepped retaining wall escorts a seasonal creek. *Courtesy of R.I. Lampus Co.*

This wall not only helps support a hillside house, it offers a tranquil spot to sit and enjoy the lake. *Courtesy of Anchor Wall Systems.*

A challenging hillside was conquered by constructing a multi-tiered retaining wall. *Courtesy of Wilson Concrete Products*

A curved retaining wall provides a level yard for children or pets. This wall also serves as a sturdy but permeable fence. *Courtesy of Rapid Building Systems.*

A retaining wall shelters a playground area. *Courtesy of Allan Block Corporation*

*Courtesy of Anchor Wall Systems*

Many retaining walls serve solely as planters to brighten up a yard.
*Courtesy of Anchor Wall Systems.*

This retaining wall runs the length of the yard, providing a platform for a fence, and a cozy oasis for birds and other wildlife. *Courtesy of Allan Block Corporation*

*Courtesy of Anchor Wall Systems*

Retaining walls serve many functions; in this case, as a decorative planter.
*Courtesy of Anchor Wall Systems*

Different shaped and sized blocks fit together to form an attractive retaining wall with plenty of space for gardening. *Courtesy of Allan Block Corporation*

Raised planters soften a rectangular patio. *Courtesy of Allan Block Corporation*

*Courtesy of Allan Block Corporation*

*Courtesy of Allan Block Corporation*

A retaining wall makes this outdoor patio a private spot to entertain.
*Courtesy of Allan Block Corporation*

A retaining wall surrounds this residential pool and creates bench seating.
*Courtesy of Kirchner Brick and Block, Inc.*

Unique white capstones finish off an attractive retaining wall, which presents a family home nicely. *Courtesy of Allan Block Corporation.*

Retaining walls can be used to redesign a hillside or yard and add raised space for planting. *Courtesy of Kirchner Brick and Block Inc.*

These units are designed to have an older, antiquated feel. The red flowers add contrast. *Courtesy of Anchor Wall Systems*

*Photo by Alexander Patho Photography*

Prominent stone steps divide a decoratively planted retaining wall. *Courtesy of R.I. Lampus Co.*

*Courtesy of Allan Block Corporation*

*Courtesy of Allan Block Corporation*

*Courtesy of Risi Stone Systems.*

*Courtesy of Innovative Concrete Design.*

Broad steps are accented by multi-level retaining walls which incorporate plants. *Courtesy of Allan Block Corporation*

A tall retaining wall keeps this swimming pool protected and adds space for additional gardening. *Courtesy of Keystone Retaining Wall Systems, Inc.*

A retaining wall surrounds this residential pool and creates bench seating. *Courtesy of Kirchner Brick and Block, Inc.*

Matching the inclination of the steps, these terraced walls define the entrance. *Courtesy of Anchor Wall Systems*

*Courtesy of Wilson Concrete Products*

*Courtesy of Anchor Wall Systems*

This attractive retaining wall offers abundant space for placing sculptures, flower pots, and even flower and plant beds. Additionally, it separates the yard into different levels to add variety. *Courtesy of Wilson Concrete Products*

Stairs built into this retaining wall provide easy access to the footpath up above.
*Courtesy of Risi Stone Systems*

This colorful wall serves as a fence, or an attractive property boundary.
*Courtesy of Allan Block Corporation*

This design incorporates units with built-in lighting fixtures with this retaining wall and patio. *Courtesy of Anchor Wall Systems*

*Photo by Alexander Patho Photography*

*Courtesy of R.I. Lampus Co.*

*Courtesy of Pacific Precast Products*

*Courtesy of Allan Block Corporation*

Circular stone steps come between these curved retaining walls
which support an iron fence. *Courtesy of Allan Block Corporation*

This wall creates a decorative slant for an outdoor living space.
*Courtesy of Anchor Wall Systems*

A uniquely shaped retaining wall arcs to make room for planting.
The flat capstones provide spaces for potted plants as well.
*Courtesy of Anchor Wall Systems*

*Courtesy of Anchor Wall Systems*

*Right:*
A beautifully landscaped retaining wall makes a strong statement
for the relaxing oasis above. *Courtesy of Risi Stone Systems*

*Photo by Alexander Patho Photography*

A retaining wall defines a pool area and offers additional seating. *Courtesy of R.I. Lampus Co.*

The retaining wall being built around this pool will provide additional seating and a place to put cold drinks or hors d'oeurves. *Courtesy of Wilson Concrete Products*

*Courtesy of Keystone Retaining Wall Systems, Inc.*

This retaining wall turned a sloped yard into a flat, level surface for a swimming pool and patio. *Courtesy of Anchor Wall Systems*

Retaining walls create level living spaces; in this case, a raised patio and fence. *Courtesy of Versa-Lok.*

A retaining wall creates a raised platform for a circular patio.
*Courtesy of Allan Block Corporation*

Without this retaining wall in place to create living space, a steep, limiting hill would be all the landscapers had to work with. *Courtesy of Tensar Earth Technologies*

Some might find this wall doubles as a handrail as they descend the steps from the driveway to the yard. *Courtesy of Innovative Concrete Design.*

A mix of color and texture provides a pleasant descent for a raised backyard patio. *Courtesy of Allan Block Corporation*

A cold drink and good company are the only elements missing from this serene sunken patio. *Courtesy of Allan Block Corporation*

This wall encircles a sunken patio, perfect for entertaining. *Courtesy of Allan Block Corporation*

Courtesy of Anchor Wall Systems

This interesting layout makes a driveway more attractive. The brightly colored flowers accent the wall. *Courtesy of Rapid Building Systems.*

*Left & Above:*
The contours of this retaining wall/garden/walkway add style and depth to this curving driveway.
*Courtesy of Risi Stone Systems*

A brick facade paver walk, driveway, and a segmental retaining wall unite for a welcoming effect. *Courtesy of Anchor Wall Systems*

The curves of this basket-weave patterned wall guide motorists into their garage.
*Courtesy of Wilson Concrete Products*

Two levels were constructed on this retaining wall, allowing for a colorful flowerbed next to the stairs.
*Courtesy of Rapid Building Systems.*

A steep hillside becomes a scenic background with a decoratively planted retaining wall. *Courtesy of Pacific Precast Products*

A house on a hillside is handsomely displayed with a series of fence-capped retaining walls with stairs leading up from the driveway below. *Courtesy of Tensar Earth Technologies*

Steps built into this retaining wall provide an attractive entryway to this home. *Courtesy of Tensar Earth Technologies*

119

*Courtesy of Tensar Earth Technologies*

*Photo by Alexander Patho Photography*

*Courtesy of R.I. Lampus Co.*

A raised planter by an entryway window provides security, creating a too-obvious platform for would-be peepers. *Courtesy of Allan Block Corporation*

A retaining wall complete with flowering shrubs can replace the need for curtains for the downstairs at this split-level home. *Courtesy of Allan Block Corporation.*

*Courtesy of Allan Block Corporation*

*Courtesy of Tensar Earth Technologies*

*Right:*
The same capstones which appear on the retaining wall were used on these wide steps for consistency and style. *Courtesy of Versa-Lok*

Retaining walls are often utilized when slopes and changing elevations require walkways and steps. *Courtesy of Rockwood Retaining Walls.*

Retaining wall blocks are available in various designs and colors which enrich the landscaping theme. *Courtesy of Rockwood Retaining Walls.*

A developer utilized retaining walls to maintain consistency in a residential neighborhood. *Courtesy of Anchor Wall Systems.*

*Courtesy of Anchor Wall Systems*

# References

1. Collin, J.G. (2002, 1997) ed., *Design Manual for Segmental Retaining Walls (NCMA DMSRW)*, second edition, National Concrete Masonry Association, Herndon, VA.

2. Collin, J.G., Berg, R.R., and Meyers, M. (2002), *Segmental Retaining Wall Drainage Manual (NCMA SRWDM),* National Concrete Masonry Association, Herndon, VA.

3. Koerner, R.M. (1998), *Designing with Geosynthetics,* Prentice-Hall, Englewood Cliffs, NJ Fourth Edition (1998), 761 p.

4. Holtz, R.D., and Kovacs, W.D. (1981), *An Introduction to Geotechnical Engineering,* Prentice-Hall, Englewood Cliffs, NJ, 733 p.

5. Segmental Retaining Wall Installation Guide, National Concrete Masonry Association, third printing, 2000.

6. Goldsmith, W., M. Silva and C. Fischenich, *"Determining Optimum Degree of Soil Compaction for Balancing Mechanical Stability and Plant Growth Capacity."* ERDC-TN-EMRRP-SR-26. US Army Engineering Research and Development Center, Vicksburg, MS. 2001.

7. Gray, D.H. and R. Sotir, *Biotechnical and Soil Bioengineering Slope Stabilization.* John Wiley & Sons, New York, NY. 1996

8. Geosynthetic Research Institute, *Geosynthetic Materials,* http://www.drexel.edu/gri/gmat.html

9. Simac, M.R., Bathurst, R.J., and berg, R.R. (1993) Design Manual for Segmental Retaining Walls, first edition, National Concrete Masonry Association, Herndon, VA.

10. Concrete Paver Certification, fourth edition, Interlocking Concrete Pavement Institute, Washington, D.C.

11. NCMA TEK 8-2A, Removal of Stains from Concrete Masonry, National Concrete Masonry Association, Herndon, VA.

12. NCMA TEK 8-3A, Control and Removal of Efflorescence, National Concrete Masonry Association, Herndon, VA.

13. NCMA TEK 8-1A, Maintenance of Concrete Masonry Walls, National Concrete Masonry Association, Herndon, VA.

14. Vibromax (2001), "Understanding Soil Compaction". Vibromax American, Racine, WI, 19 p.

# Contributors

**The following companies contributed financially toward text development and programs, and/or provided images**

National Concrete Masonry Association
13750 Sunrise Valley Drive
Herndon, VA  20171
703-713-1900
www.ncma.org

Anchor Wall Systems, Inc.
5959 Baker Road, Suite 390
Minnetonka, Minnesota 55345
952-933-8855
www.anchorwall.com

Innovative Concrete Design Corporation
3934 North Ridgefield Circle
Milwaukee, Wisconsin 53211
414-962-4065
www.selecticd.com

Keystone Retaining Wall Systems, Inc.
4444 West 78th Street
Minneapolis, MN 55435
952-897-1040
www.keystonewalls.com

Kirchner Block and Brick Inc.
12901 St. Charles Rock Road
Bridgeton, Missouri 63044
314-291-3200
www.kirchnerblock.com

Rockwood Retaining Walls, Inc.
325 Alliance Place N.E.
Rochester, Minnesota 55906
507-529-2871
www.retainingwall.com

R.I. Lampus Company
816 R.I. Lampus Avenue
PO Box 167
Springdale, PA 15144
412-362-3800
www.lampus.com

Risi Stone Systems
8500 Leslie Street, Suite 390
Thornhill, ON Canada
L3T 7M8
905-882-5898
www.risistone.com

Wilson Concrete Products
10075 Sheehan Road
Centerville, OH 45458
866-885-7965
www.wilsonconcreteproducts.com

Versa-Lok Retaining Wall Systems
6348 Hwy 36 Blvd., Suite 1
Oakdale, MN 55128
651-770-3166
www.versa-lok.com

Barnes & Cone, Inc.
5894 Court Street Road
Syracuse, NY 13206
315-437-0305
www.barnesandcone.com

Basalite Concrete Products, LLC
605 Industrial Way
Dixon, CA 95620
707-678-1901
www.basalite.com

Binkley & Ober, Inc.
Route 72 North
East Petersburg, PA 17520
717-569-0441
www.binkleyandober.com

Chicago Block & Brick Company
PO Box 388199
Chicago, IL 60638
708-458-8130

CTI, Inc./Masa-USA LLC
2231 Holmgren Way
Green Bay, WI 54304
www.CTI5050.com

Featherlite Building Products
2824 Real Street
Austin, TX 78722
512-472-2424
www.featherlitetexas.com

Fendt Builders Supply, Inc.
22005 Gill Road
Farmington Hills, MI 48335
248-474-3211
www.fendtproducts.com

RCP Block & Brick, Inc.
8240 Broadway
Lemon Grove, CA 91945
619-460-7520
www.rcpblock.com

Rekers (NA), Inc.
175 Clearbrook Road
Elmsford, NY 10523
914-347-7446
www.rekers.com

Ten Cate Nicolon
365 South Holland Drive
Pendergrass, GA 30567
706-693-2226
www.tcnicolon.com

W.R. Grace & Co.
62 Whittemore Avenue
Cambridge, MA 02140
617-876-1400
www.graceconstruction.com

**The following companies provided images:**

Allan Block Corporation
5300 Edina Industrial Blvd, Suite 100
Edina, Minnesota 55439
952-835-5309
www.allanblock.com

Pacific Precast Products, Ltd.
937 Fresno Place
Coquitlam, British Columbia
V3J 6G5 Canada
604-939-7999
www.pacificprecast.com

Rapid Building System
PO Box 3335
Reston, Virginia 20195
703-471-4082
www.rapidbuilding.com

Tensar Earth Technologies, Inc.
5883 Glenridge Drive, Suite 200
Atlanta, Georgia 30328
1-800-TENSAR-1
www.tensarcorp.com